W9-CAZ-289

254

Benjamin Davis, Jr.

Catherine Reef

Twenty-First Century Books

A Division of Henry Holt and Co., Inc.
Frederick, Maryland

PHOTO CREDITS

cover: flag by Fred J. Eckert/FPG International; portrait courtesy of the National Archives.
3: National Archives. **4:** courtesy of the United States Military Academy. **9:** Library of Congress.
13: Library of Congress.
15: Bettmann. **19:** Bern Keating/ Black Star. **20:** FPG International.
22: Smithsonian Institution.
23: UPI/Bettmann. **28:** The Schomburg Center for Research in Black Culture. **29:** Bettmann.
31: Bettmann. **32:** UPI/Bettmann.
34: courtesy of the United States Military Academy. **38:** UPI/ Bettmann. **43:** UPI/Bettmann.
45: National Archives.
46-47: Smithsonian Institution.
50: Smithsonian Institution.
51: Smithsonian Institution.
52: Smithsonian Institution.
55: Smithsonian Institution.
57: National Archives.
59: National Archives.
62: Smithsonian Institution.
64: National Archives. **66:** UPI/ Bettmann. **67:** UPI/Bettmann.
71: UPI/Bettmann. **73:** UPI/ Bettmann. **74:** National Archives.

Published by
Twenty-First Century Books
A Division of Henry Holt and Co., Inc.
38 South Market Street
Frederick, Maryland 21701

Text Copyright © 1992
Catherine Reef

Printed in Mexico
10 9 8 7 6 5 4 3 2 1

Library of Congress Cataloging in Publication Data
Reef, Catherine
Benjamin Davis, Jr.
(An African-American Soldiers Book)
Includes bibliographical references and index.
Summary: Examines the life of Benjamin Davis, Jr., the first black man to graduate from West Point in the twentieth century, who pursued his chosen course of a military career despite the prejudice against him.
1. Davis, Benjamin O. (Benjamin Oliver), 1912- —Juvenile literature. 2. Generals—United States—Biography—Juvenile literature.
3. United States. Air Force—Biography—Juvenile literature.
4. Afro-American generals—Biography—Juvenile literature.
[1. Davis, Benjamin O. (Benjamin Oliver), 1912- . 2. Generals.
3. Afro-Americans—Biography.] I. Title. II. Series: African-American Soldiers.
UG626.2.D37R44 1992 358.4'0092—dc20 [B] 91-43504 CIP AC
ISBN 0-8050-2137-X

Contents

Chapter 1

Proving Himself

It was November, and all along New York's Hudson River, trees were dropping their red and brown leaves. It was an exciting time for the men of the U.S. Military Academy at West Point. They were looking forward to football games and Christmas vacation. The older students were thinking about graduation and their careers as Army officers.

Benjamin O. Davis, Jr., knew what career he wanted. He wanted to be a pilot. As the tall, slim cadet walked toward the superintendent's office on a chilly day in 1935, Davis was confident that his application to join the Army Air Corps would be accepted. After all, he had earned excellent grades at West Point and received a high rating on his physical examination.

Benjamin Davis, Jr., posed for this yearbook portrait in 1936.

But when Davis reached the office of Major General William D. Connor, the superintendent of West Point, he received some unexpected, and unwelcomed, news. Connor handed the young man a letter from the assistant chief of the Army Air Corps. It said that the cadet's application had been rejected. Benjamin Davis could not join the Air Corps because he was black.

"I had been rejected because no black units were to be included in the Air Corps," Davis later recalled. "The decision, which came as a complete shock to me, was shameless."

Superintendent Connor urged Davis to choose a different career. Connor warned the disappointed cadet that this rejection was only the first of many problems that he would face in the Army because of his race. A black officer would not be permitted to learn such a difficult task as flying a plane. A black officer would not be allowed to command white troops.

Davis should have realized that this was true. His own father had endured years of prejudice as an Army officer. Benjamin O. Davis, Sr., had been denied military assignments for which he was clearly qualified. But the younger Davis had thought that his career would be different. "Even the great

U.S. Army," he had believed, "could not afford to turn down the services of a highly qualified West Point graduate who was eager to serve his country in the Air Corps."

Connor sat Davis down and gave him some advice. He suggested that the young man apply for an Army assignment near a university. That way, Davis could attend law school and work as a lawyer after leaving the Army. With his sharp mind, Davis could even run for Congress some day, the superintendent said.

Davis understood that Connor was trying to be helpful. "He was being completely honest and truly believed everything he suggested was in my interest," Davis said. There was one thing wrong with Connor's plan, however. Davis had no interest in law school or politics. "I was still determined to fly airplanes," he stated.

Years later, Benjamin Davis said that Connor had done him a favor. "He brought out my stubborn streak," Davis remarked. "My decision to continue on my chosen course was largely based on pure obstinacy—a determination to prove my worth."

In his need to prove his abilities, Davis was like the thousands of other African-American soldiers who have served, over the years, in the U.S.

"My decision to continue on my chosen course was largely based on pure obstinacy—a determination to prove my worth."

military. Black men and women have taken part in every American war, from the Revolutionary War in the 1770s to the Persian Gulf War in 1991. And each war has brought a new and separate battle for America's black soldiers—a battle to overcome racial discrimination. Each war has brought a new struggle to gain the same opportunities offered to white soldiers.

Benjamin Davis, Jr., had to prove himself at every step of his career. At West Point, he lived through four years of unfair and harsh treatment to become only the fourth African American to graduate from the military academy in its history—and the first black cadet to graduate in the twentieth century.

He had to prove his abilities again in 1941, when the United States began a training program for black fighter pilots. At the Tuskegee Army Air Field in Alabama, Davis at last learned to fly. The Army placed him in command of the country's first African-American combat pilots.

Davis demanded excellence from these men, knowing that many white Americans thought that blacks could not fly planes. He explained, "We were embarking on an adventure that could make an enormous difference for the future of black airmen."

The pilots who trained on that Alabama airfield became known as the Tuskegee Airmen. In World War II, they earned a reputation for bravery and skill, and their wartime performance gained blacks a permanent role in military aviation. The success of the Tuskegee Airmen also helped to end racial segregation in America's armed forces.

Davis's military career continued after World War II. He went on to command troops—both

Davis stands next to his plane during World War II.

black and white—in nations throughout the world. His efforts helped to support American troops as they fought in Korea and Vietnam.

Benjamin O. Davis, Jr., retired from the U.S. Air Force in 1970, having reached the rank of major general. He did not stop working for his country, though. "I had welcomed challenges all my life," he stated. Davis continued to welcome them after he retired from the military. He went to work for the Department of Transportation in Washington, D.C., to improve the safety of the nation's skies and roadways.

Wherever they were stationed, Davis and his wife, Agatha, got to know the people of the country in which they lived—"people who were different in appearance and culture from Americans," Davis noted, "but who had the same aspirations." Overseas, race was not a barrier to equal opportunity. In other countries, people came to know Benjamin Davis not as a black man, but as a human being— and the contrast with his treatment at home was often painful.

Throughout a long career, Davis has seen many black Americans overcome racism to achieve their goals, in both military and civilian life. Yet he sees, too, that racism continues to harm the lives of all

Americans. "It is a cancer, really, on our society," he says. "And it is one that will have to be eased beyond the point that it has already been eased if our society is to be a happier one than it is today."

"The future of this nation," says Benjamin O. Davis, Jr., "is largely dependent on how Americans treat each other."

Chapter 2

A Soldier's Son

Six-year-old Benjamin O. Davis, Jr., saw many changes as he rode the streetcars of Washington, D.C. The year was 1919. Government buildings were springing up in the heart of the city. Beside the Potomac River, workers were laboring on a great stone monument to Abraham Lincoln.

The young boy saw changes on his own busy street, where ice men and grocers made deliveries from horse-drawn wagons. "I remember Katzman's Grocery on the corner of 11th and T streets," he recalled, "and the excitement in the neighborhood when Mr. Katzman converted his delivery wagon to the first motor-driven truck I had ever seen."

The population of Washington was changing, too. During World War I, thousands of people had moved to the nation's capital looking for work. Among them were many black Americans who had come from farming communities in the South.

There never seemed to be enough housing for the new arrivals. Now that the war had ended and soldiers were returning home, jobs were also hard to find.

That summer, riots broke out in Washington and other cities. Many white Americans were afraid that they would lose their jobs to black workers. That fear led white soldiers and sailors to attack black citizens on the streets of the nation's capital.

The fighting lasted for several days. A white mob moved through the city, looking for fights with blacks. In neighborhoods where black people

A young Benjamin Davis rode electric streetcars in Washington, D.C.

lived, whites were attacked. Some men even fought with the guns they had brought home from World War I.

In the house at 1830 11th Street, Benjamin received a warning from his aunt: stay away from U Street. "I heard real fear in the voices of my cousins and my aunt when they talked about the 'race riots on U Street,'" he recalled. Benjamin and his sisters, Olive and Elnora, stayed safely away.

The house on 11th Street was the home of Louis and Henrietta Davis, Benjamin's grand-parents. Benjamin was born there on December 12, 1912. In 1919, the Davis children were living with their grandparents. Their father, an officer in the U.S. Army, was serving in the Philippines, a group of islands in Southeast Asia. (Elnora Dick-erson Davis, Benjamin's mother, had died in 1916.)

With many aunts, uncles, and cousins nearby, Benjamin seldom felt lonely in Washington. His Uncle Ernest took him on streetcar rides, and his Aunt Lyd taught him how to make root beer. On Sundays, he visited his Uncle Louis and Aunt Ruth, who lived in the country with their nine children.

The city child enjoyed his days on the farm. "I always looked forward to the Sunday feast of homegrown vegetables and homemade ice cream and cake," Davis remembered. Benjamin pitched hay, swam in the farm's swimming hole, and rode a burro named Tipperary.

A calm and serious boy, Benjamin Davis did not grow frightened when Tipperary bit him one day. According to the family story, Benjamin bit him back!

In May 1920, Benjamin's father, Colonel Benjamin O. Davis, Sr., returned to Washington. The sight of his father in an Army uniform filled the boy with pride. "My father was all Army, through and through," Benjamin observed. "He had always wanted to be a soldier."

Colonel Davis had come home with his new wife, Sadie. Young Benjamin and his sisters already knew and loved the woman they called Mother Sadie. Sadie Overton was an old family friend. She and Colonel Davis were married in the Philippines in December 1919.

Colonel Davis brought his family to Alabama, where the Army had given him a new assignment. He was to teach military science and tactics at the Tuskegee Institute. Booker T. Washington, a well-known educator, had founded this school in 1881 to teach Southern blacks the practical skills that would enable them to better themselves.

Booker T. Washington founded the Tuskegee Institute in 1881.

Colonel Davis would have preferred to train and command combat troops. But at the time, the U.S. Army was strictly segregated. A black officer would not be assigned to a position of command over white soldiers, and black soldiers were mostly given non-combat assignments, such as camp maintenance. Such policies had limited the colonel's opportunities throughout his military career.

As a young man, Benjamin Davis, Sr., wanted to become an officer in the U.S. Army. Unable to get an appointment to West Point, the senior Davis enlisted in the Army in 1889 as an ordinary soldier. He was assigned to the 9th Cavalry, an all-black unit stationed at Fort Duchesne, Utah. In 1901, the senior Davis did become an officer—one of only two black Army officers at that time.

At the turn of the century, Benjamin's father was ordered to the Philippines following a revolt against American control of the islands. From 1912 to 1915, during the Mexican Revolution, he served on the U.S. border with Mexico.

Davis was again stationed in the Philippines during World War I, when the United States and other nations fought against Germany. He wanted to take part in the war in Europe, but the Army would not grant his request.

By the time the Davises settled at the Tuskegee Institute, Colonel Davis was the only black officer in the Army. His determination was an impressive lesson for a growing boy. "How lucky I was," young Benjamin believed, "to have a father who, in spite of formidable obstacles, would fight for his beliefs and ambitions and win!"

The Davis family enjoyed a pleasant life at Tuskegee. "I liked everything I saw in my new home," Benjamin remembered. Colonel and Mrs. Davis ran their household in strict military fashion. According to their son, "We arrived on time for meals, sat up straight at the table, and ate all the food on our plates." Benjamin and his sisters observed the household rules. "There was no such thing as talking back," Benjamin said.

A professor of English before her marriage to Colonel Davis, Mother Sadie shared her love of learning with the children. She arranged for Olive, the oldest child, to attend a high school in Atlanta, Georgia. There, Sadie believed, Olive would be well prepared for a college education.

Mother Sadie hung lamps over the children's beds so that Benjamin and Elnora could read before falling asleep. "I was also given school achievement goals," Benjamin recalled, "and only excellence in

"How lucky I was to have a father who, in spite of formidable obstacles, would fight for his beliefs and ambitions and win!"

performance was acceptable." If Benjamin's grades were in the 90s, Mother Sadie would ask, "Why were they not 100?"

The growing boy thrived in this strict setting. "I could appreciate what was being done for us," he wrote years later. "I was happy with the Davis method."

At Tuskegee, the Davis family lived away from the world of prejudice that surrounded the Institute. But the college's boundaries could not protect the Davises from the hatred of their white neighbors. "The fact of racism was forced upon us whenever we left the Institute," Benjamin said. Many shopkeepers in the nearby city of Montgomery would not sell their goods to black customers. Other store owners waited on white customers first.

Throughout the South, young Benjamin saw signs of Jim Crow laws—laws requiring separate public facilities for whites and blacks. There were separate schools, restaurants, and movie theaters; there were "white" and "black" rest rooms and even drinking fountains. The U.S. Supreme Court had ruled in 1896 that this kind of segregation was legal as long as the facilities were "separate but equal." But the facilities that were provided for blacks were almost always inferior.

When Benjamin Davis, Jr., was growing up, Jim Crow laws required blacks to use separate entrances at movie theaters.

Some southern whites belonged to groups such as the Ku Klux Klan, which believed that white people were superior to blacks. Not long after the Davises arrived in Tuskegee, the Klan announced plans to march past the Institute. "It is difficult to appreciate fully the terror the Klan created in the minds of black people," Davis noted. The white-robed Klan members were known for their record of violence against blacks.

The Ku Klux Klan tried to frighten blacks and other minorities.

The Institute's residents received instructions for the night of the march: turn your lights off, stay inside, and don't draw attention to yourself. Once again, Benjamin was warned to stay away from the scene of trouble.

Those instructions were meant to keep people safe, but they did not sit well with Benjamin O. Davis, Sr. "My father felt very strongly that he, as a Regular Army colonel, should not permit himself to be intimidated by the members of the Ku Klux Klan," the younger Davis recalled. "He believed

20

that the entire Davis family should make known its opinion of the Klan by staying visible and not hiding in the shadows."

Colonel Davis put on his white dress uniform and turned on the outdoor light. "Our porch light was the only light to be seen for miles around except for the flaming torches of the Klansmen," Benjamin later wrote. As the family stood on the porch and watched the parade of white-robed Klansmen, Benjamin Davis, Jr., learned that he did not have to hide from racism.

In the summer of 1926, Colonel Davis and Mother Sadie traveled to Europe with Olive, who had just graduated from high school. "My father was always happiest overseas," Davis said, "where black people were treated far better than they were by most of their own countrymen at home." Benjamin and Elnora spent the summer with relatives in Washington, D.C.

One Sunday, Benjamin's Uncle Ernest took the 13-year-old boy to Bolling Field. On that stretch of bare earth, daredevil pilots called barnstormers thrilled crowds with their airborne stunts.

Since Wilbur and Orville Wright made the first airplane flight in 1903, airplanes had captured the public's imagination. Soon, adventurous pilots

Daredevil pilots called barnstormers entertained Benjamin Davis with their airborne shows.

set records for the longest non-stop flights—from Chicago to New York, from New York to Alaska, from Florida to California. Barnstormers traveled from place to place, giving dramatic shows of their airborne acrobatics.

The sight of a barnstormer diving and looping through the air filled Benjamin with excitement. As an adult, Benjamin could still remember "the airplane taking off into the clear blue sky, the thrill of seeing it climb to altitude, make its breathtaking maneuvers, and finally return to earth."

After Colonel Davis returned from Europe, he took his son back to Bolling Field. This time, young Benjamin did more than simply stand and watch the planes in the sky. Colonel Davis paid one of the barnstormers to take the boy for a ride. "I can only guess that he was looking far into the future," Benjamin said, "and, seeing airplanes in that future, realized in some mysterious way that I would benefit from the experience."

Excitedly, Benjamin slipped goggles over his eyes and climbed into the open cockpit. As the plane rose into the sky and turned sharply, Benjamin saw the pillowy clouds above and the buildings of Washington, D.C., below.

That glorious ride became a turning point in Benjamin Davis's life. "That one ride made me fall in love with airplanes and gave me the desire to be a pilot myself," he said.

At summer's end, the Davis family headed for Cleveland, Ohio, where Colonel Davis had been assigned as an instructor for a black National Guard unit. Benjamin settled into a new school and got a job delivering newspapers.

In 1927, Benjamin Davis, Jr., listened to the radio broadcasts covering Charles Lindbergh's solo flight across the Atlantic Ocean. In a journey that lasted more than 30 hours, Lindbergh flew from New York City to Paris, France, in his single-engine airplane, *The Spirit of St. Louis.* "I was gripped by the reports of his flight," Davis said. "The drama of Lindbergh's contribution seized my imagination."

In 1927, Charles Lindbergh flew solo across the Atlantic Ocean.

Benjamin graduated from Cleveland's Central High School in 1929 with the highest grades in his class. He enrolled in Western Reserve University in Cleveland, but he was not happy there.

With a college education, a black person in America could become a teacher or a lawyer, a doctor or an engineer. But those careers did not interest Benjamin Davis, Jr. "I still wanted to fly planes," he said.

Benjamin realized, though, that his ambition to fly would have to remain a dream. At that time, there was no pilot-training program that accepted black trainees. Many white Americans still believed that black people lacked the ability to learn complex technical skills. "There was considerable doubt that blacks could fly airplanes," Benjamin noted.

Colonel Davis proposed another career to Benjamin. Despite the discrimination that he had faced in the military, the senior Davis suggested that Benjamin attend West Point and become an officer in the U.S. Army.

"My father believed strongly in America," Benjamin explained. Colonel Davis felt that the United States could not be a true democracy until black people were integrated into every aspect of society. The colonel was especially "proud of the performance of blacks in America's wars from the Revolution on," Benjamin remarked, and he wanted the U.S. Army to have at least one black officer after he retired.

After an aimless year at Western Reserve, Benjamin realized that his life needed some direction. He decided to seek admission to West Point. "No matter what obstacles might present themselves," Benjamin said, "I was determined to attend West Point and pursue the career my father had chosen."

Chapter 3

Orders, Routine, Silence

The obstacles that presented themselves to Benjamin Davis were serious ones. To get into West Point, a person has to be appointed by an elected official of the U.S. government—the president, the vice president, or a U.S. senator or representative. But at that time, white officials were likely to ignore the requests of African Americans.

Only a handful of blacks had managed to gain an appointment to the academy before Benjamin Davis applied for admission. In 1877, Henry Flipper became the first black cadet to graduate from West Point, and two other black students graduated in the 1800s. There had been no African-American graduates in the twentieth century.

In 1929, the only black representative in Congress was Oscar De Priest of Illinois. Davis enrolled at the University of Chicago so that Congressman De Priest would be his representative. De Priest secured for him an appointment to the academy.

But Davis then faced another tough obstacle—West Point's entrance examination. Davis took the exam in March 1931, but he had not studied for it. He failed the test. Deeply discouraged, Davis imagined how disappointed his father would be. "I wrote my father to tell him I had failed," he said. "I apologized for letting the family down."

Colonel Davis wrote back to say that he still had faith in his son—and Benjamin still had faith in himself. He studied hard and took the exam a second time, in March 1932. This time, Benjamin passed easily.

"You have the world waiting for you," a proud Colonel Davis wrote his son when he heard the good news. He reminded Benjamin that 12 million people—the African-American population of the United States—would be watching his progress.

It pleased Colonel Davis to see Benjamin join the tradition of African-American service in the armed forces. In each of America's wars, blacks who wanted to serve in the military have struggled

Crispus Attucks, a former slave, was the first person killed in the Revolutionary War.

to overcome the barrier of racial prejudice. Even General George Washington, as the leader of the Continental Army, thought that only white men were capable of fighting for America's freedom.

Blacks had begun to die for America's independence before the Revolutionary War began. A former slave named Crispus Attucks was the first person to be killed in that struggle. He was shot when British soldiers and angry colonists clashed in the "Boston Massacre" of March 5, 1770.

By the end of the war, 7,000 black soldiers and sailors had seen battle, 5,000 in the Army and another 2,000 in the Navy. "No regiment is to be seen in which there are not Negroes in abundance," one soldier observed, "and among them are able-bodied, strong, and brave fellows."

A black soldier named Peter Salem became a hero of the Revolution when he killed the British major John Pitcairn at the Battle of Bunker Hill. Another black soldier at Bunker Hill, Salem Poor, received a citation for his "brave and gallant" fighting. Other African-American men—William Flora, James Forten, Lemuel Haynes, and others—added their names to the list of black heroes.

Black fighting men helped the United States defeat the British in the War of 1812. Again, they

had to prove their bravery and patriotism. Again, they helped to win important battles, such as the Battle of Lake Erie.

Captain Oliver Hazard Perry had been ordered to take control of Lake Erie from the British. To win the battle, he needed more men. But when reinforcements arrived, Perry was displeased. The new men were a "motley set of blacks," Captain Perry complained.

Perry's commander, Commodore Isaac Chauncey, told him that these black seamen were among the best in America's fleet. "I have yet to learn

This engraving shows Commodore Oliver Hazard Perry aboard his flagship during the Battle of Lake Erie in 1813.

29

that the color of the skin," said Chauncey, "can affect a man's qualifications and usefulness." Perry soon learned that his commander was correct. The Americans won the battle, and Perry gave special praise to his black crew members.

While blacks were welcomed and valued in times of war, they were banned from the armed forces in times of peace. In 1820, an Army order stated that "No Negro or Mulatto will be received as a recruit of the Army." (The term "mulatto" refers to a person of mixed race.) And by the time the Civil War began 41 years later, U.S. military and civilian leaders had forgotten the contributions of America's black soldiers.

At first, in this bloody conflict between the North and the South, the North enlisted only white soldiers. Again, it was suggested that black people lacked the courage and ability to fight. This angered anti-slavery leaders, including the black writer and newspaper editor Frederick Douglass, who had himself escaped from slavery. "This is no time to fight with your white hand and allow your black hand to be tied!" Douglass proclaimed.

On July 17, 1862, the U.S. Congress approved the formation of the first units of black soldiers, later known as the United States Colored Troops.

Some blacks were commissioned as officers, but the commanders of these units were white. The Army would not give black soldiers the responsibility of leading combat troops.

In more than 400 battles of the Civil War, the members of these all-black units proved their ability to fight bravely and skillfully. Thirty-eight thousand black fighting men lost their lives in the long struggle. Colonel Thomas Higginson, a white officer who commanded a regiment of freed slaves, remarked that the black soldiers "shamed the nation into recognizing them as men."

No unit brought more glory to black fighting men than the 54th Massachusetts Infantry. Their valiant assault on Fort Wagner in South Carolina, celebrated in newspapers across the country, rallied support for black troops. For his heroism at Fort Wagner, Sergeant William Carney became the first African American to earn the Congressional Medal of Honor.

Following the Civil War, the United States made black soldiers part of the peacetime Army for the first time. The Army created four regiments of black soldiers and sent them to the Western frontier to protect settlers. These regiments were known as the Buffalo Soldiers. Again, America's

African Americans, like this corporal, fought bravely in the Civil War.

black soldiers proved themselves worthy. "Everything that men could do, they did," remarked the commander of the Buffalo Soldiers.

By 1917, when the United States entered the First World War, thousands of blacks were in the armed forces. With the outbreak of war, hundreds

A black soldier wounded in World War I watches a victory parade.

of thousands of African Americans registered for military service. Black soldiers were commissioned as officers, and they began to demand the right to command combat troops.

The Army refused to consider their requests. Though several black units saw combat in France—where they won praise for their heroism—they were under the command of white officers.

Colonel Charles Young, a black officer, was well qualified to lead troops. However, rather than give Young that opportunity, the Army forced him to retire. Young had high blood pressure, Army officials claimed, and was unfit for service.

An 1899 West Point graduate, Young decided to prove his fitness for active duty. He rode a horse from Ohio to Washington, D.C.—a distance of 497 miles—in only 16 days. Colonel Young was allowed to re-enter the Army, but he was never given the chance to command troops.

Benjamin Davis, Jr., admired the courage of the black fighting men who had come before him. But the one soldier who most earned Davis's respect was his father. "He had made life easier for me. Now it was my turn to make things easier for those who would come after me," Davis said. "I was determined to succeed."

This aerial photo of West Point was taken in 1930, shortly before Benjamin Davis, Jr., was a cadet.

In July 1932, Benjamin Davis, Jr., boarded the train to West Point. As Davis looked at the green forests and blue skies outside, he wondered if the trip would ever end. "I felt lucky to be alive," he wrote, "at the beginning of what promised to be the greatest adventure of my life so far."

He thought about the friends he would make. He imagined what it would be like to live by the academy's motto: "Duty, Honor, Country."

At last, Davis arrived at West Point. He and the other new cadets were shown to their rooms.

Although most of the other cadets had roommates, Davis roomed alone. No white cadets would be asked to room with him, the commandant of cadets explained. "It was hard for me to believe that West Point could take such a stand," Davis recalled. "It did not seem consistent with the 'Duty, Honor, Country' creed I had read about."

On Davis's third night at West Point, someone knocked on the door of his room. A voice invited him to a meeting in the basement. The meeting had already begun when Davis reached the basement. As he approached the gathered cadets, he heard one ask, "What are we going to do about the nigger?"

Nearly 60 years later, Davis said, "I can hear that question at this very moment." Davis hurried back to his room. From that night on, the other cadets "silenced" him. They spoke to him only in the line of duty.

Usually, cadets received this treatment if they broke West Point's honor code—if they cheated on a test, for example. But Benjamin Davis was silenced simply because he was black.

For four years at West Point, Davis was, in his words, an "invisible man." He sat alone on buses traveling to football games. Table assignments in the mess hall constantly changed because so many cadets would not eat with him. "This cruel treatment was designed to make me buckle," Davis understood, "but I refused to buckle in any way. I maintained my self-respect."

Davis found ways to cope with his solitary life. "I bolstered my feelings by thinking that they were missing a great deal by not knowing me," he said. Davis settled into the strict routine at West Point. He studied history, science, and mathematics. He trained to be a soldier, marching in practice parades and taking courses in field artillery, signal corps, and riding. "Soon I found myself adjusting to the situation and able to concentrate on doing my work well," Davis remarked.

During the Christmas vacation of his second year at West Point, Davis attended a New Year's Eve dance in New York City. To his surprise, a young woman stuffed a handful of confetti down the back of his coat. "There was this handsome guy in a West Point uniform," recalled the woman, whose name was Agatha Scott, "and all the girls in the place were after him. But I decided he was going to pay attention to me."

That summer, Benjamin saw Agatha again. He learned that she was a teacher from New Haven,

Connecticut. The two met again during Benjamin's next Christmas break. "Upon my return to West Point, I wrote my father that I was very much in love with her," Benjamin said.

Agatha began to visit Benjamin at West Point every Saturday. "She experienced the same silence I did on these afternoons," Davis recalled, "but we were happy despite our isolation and did not need anyone else." The couple spent hours together in West Point's library. "Not that we looked at the books," Agatha said. "We looked at each other."

Davis had begun to think about his career. He decided to apply to the Army Air Corps despite the fact that it had no black units at the time. But the Air Corps did not want a black officer. "It was not 'logical' for a black officer to command white troops," General William Connor, the superintendent of West Point, told Davis. He advised the young man to give up his dream of flying.

Davis was determined to follow only one career path. In the meantime, however, he decided to go wherever the Army sent him. "I still thought it possible and reasonable," he explained, "that under different conditions, in a future no one could confidently forecast, I might command white troops and fly an Army airplane."

With that hope, Benjamin Davis, Jr., graduated from the academy in June 1936. Two weeks later, he and Agatha were married in the West Point chapel. "None too soon," Benjamin Davis said, "I left behind the orders, the routine, and the silence I had endured for four years."

Benjamin Davis, Sr., congratulates his son on graduation day.

Chapter 4

Flying

Benjamin Davis was soon learning a new set of rules. As he and Agatha drove to Fort Benning, Georgia, they studied the "Hints of Behavior"—the rules of social etiquette that officers and their wives were expected to follow. They wanted to do everything correctly when they arrived at the military post where Davis had been assigned.

The "Hints of Behavior" told the Davises that they were expected to pay calls on the commanding officer and the other officers on the base. Davis, now an Army second lieutenant, was also supposed to join Fort Benning's officers' club.

At that time, segregation made car trips for black people difficult in the South. Unwelcome in most of the hotels that they passed, Benjamin and Agatha had to sleep in their car. They were unable to find rest rooms that they were permitted to use.

The Davises knew that they would face these inconveniences while traveling, but they did not expect unequal treatment once they arrived at Fort Benning. Yet they soon learned, as Davis observed, that "the silence continued."

The other officers chose to ignore the "Hints of Behavior" when dealing with the black couple. The commanding officer pretended to be out when the Davises came to call. Davis's application to join the officers' club was returned in the mail. Shunned by white colleagues and neighbors, the Davises turned to each other for friendship and support. They would not permit racial prejudice "to detract from our happiness," Davis said.

Davis's work assignment at Fort Benning was disappointing, too. He worked with Company F, a black unit commanded by a white officer. "In those days," Davis noted, "black troops were trained not for combat but for 'service'—maintaining equipment and grounds, janitorial service for officers' quarters, cleaning stables."

In September 1937, Benjamin Davis entered Fort Benning's Infantry School, where he learned the fighting strategies used by foot soldiers. He and the other students studied the war tactics of both present-day armies and those from the past. The

"More than anything else, I wanted to be regarded with the respect due a Regular Army officer."

following spring, the Infantry School students were to receive their new orders, and Davis looked forward to learning what his would be.

Officers with Davis's skills and training usually received assignments commanding troops. "More than anything else, I wanted to be regarded with the respect due a Regular Army officer," Davis said. "I wanted to earn that respect through performance and demonstrated ability."

However, Davis's new assignment turned out to be another setback. He was given the job that his father had held for so many years: professor of military science and tactics at the Tuskegee Institute. "It appeared that General Connor had been correct in his judgment that there would be no real career for me in the Army," a disappointed Davis remarked.

"As close to nothing as it could be and still be called a job"—that's how Davis described his position at Tuskegee. He gave three short lectures each week and had nothing to do for the rest of the time.

Although he had been promoted to captain, it seemed to Benjamin Davis that his military career had come to an end. But there was little chance of starting a career in another field. The nation was in the midst of the Great Depression, a time of severe economic hardship, and jobs of any kind were hard to find.

In September 1940, Davis received welcome news. His father had been promoted to brigadier general. Benjamin Davis, Sr., had become the first black general in the history of the United States. "My father had richly deserved it for many years," the younger Davis said. General Davis was assigned to Fort Riley, Kansas, where he would command the 9th and 10th cavalry regiments. He requested that his son be assigned to serve as his aide. For Benjamin Davis, Jr., "things were definitely changing for the better."

Events overseas were changing things for all Americans. Having marched across the countries of eastern Europe, the German army was preparing for attacks on England and France. World War II had begun. Although the United States chose to remain neutral, many military leaders believed that it would be impossible to stay out of the war for long. President Franklin D. Roosevelt decided to ready the American armed forces for war.

Under pressure from the National Association for the Advancement of Colored People and other civil rights groups, the president announced the

President Franklin D. Roosevelt prepared the United States for war as German forces attacked England and France.

formation of a black flying unit. The commander of this new unit—to be known as the 99th Pursuit Squadron—was to be Benjamin O. Davis, Jr. In 1941, Davis received his orders to report for flight training. He could hardly believe his good fortune.

For the Army, the pilot training at Tuskegee was an experiment. Davis himself called the Tuskegee program a "high-stakes" gamble. As he knew, the future role of African Americans in the U.S. military would be determined by the performance of black soldiers during the war.

In the spring of 1941, Benjamin Davis reported to the Tuskegee Army Air Field, located near the Tuskegee Institute. The government had created this new airfield especially to train black pilots. The segregated Army would not allow blacks and whites to train together.

Segregation was a problem for the cadets at Tuskegee. The Army provided separate facilities and living quarters for the black cadets and white instructors. By conforming to local customs, Army officials hoped to avoid arousing anger in the nearby communities.

The cadets were angry and resentful, but Davis reminded them of the importance of their mission. "My own opinion was that blacks could best over-

During World War II, African Americans studied aviation at the Tuskegee Army Air Field.

come racist attitudes through their achievements," Davis explained, "even though those achievements had to take place within the hateful environment of segregation."

By August 1941, the Tuskegee cadets had completed their classroom training. They were ready to learn to fly. "The eyes of your country and the eyes of your people are on you," a visiting general told them.

Benjamin Davis, Jr., 28 years old, discovered that flying was as joyous as he had thought it would

be. "It was summer in Alabama," Davis wrote, "and flying over the green trees, the streams, and the orderly plots of farmland below was more exhilarating than anything I could have imagined."

At first, the cadets flew with an instructor in the back seat. By September, they were ready to take their planes up alone. "This is what I had been waiting for," Davis said. "It was my airplane."

A base commander reviews the first class of Tuskegee aviators in 1941.

Davis and the others spent seven months at the controls of a "lumbering" BT-13, mastering the art of precision flying. He loved all of the maneuvers—the stalls and loops, the forced landings and vertical reverses, the slow rolls and inverted flights.

Every flight was exciting for Davis. "I always felt a first surge of exhilaration when I climbed into the cockpit," he wrote, "another when I pushed the throttle forward for takeoff, and yet another when I was airborne." Flying, Davis had discovered, was "one great feeling."

On December 7, 1941, Benjamin Davis, Jr., was having dinner when he heard the news that Japanese planes had attacked the American naval base at Pearl Harbor, Hawaii. The United States had entered World War II. The cadets at Tuskegee knew that they would soon be called upon to fight.

The Tuskegee Airmen were going to war.

On March 7, 1942, Davis and the other cadets who had completed their flight training received their wings. They were pilots—the first African-American pilots—in the U.S. Army Air Corps. But Davis knew that the men of the 99th had yet to be tested—and had yet to prove themselves. Only combat would allow these airmen to demonstrate their skills.

Benjamin Davis also knew that the success or failure of the 99th would affect the lives of other black fighting men. "If a black fighter squadron could give a good account of itself in combat," Davis pointed out, "its success might lead the way to greater opportunities for black people throughout the armed services."

Chapter 5

Meeting the Challenge

The pilots of the 99th Pursuit Squadron had to wait for their combat orders. According to Benjamin Davis, the men of the 99th "used the time getting ready and keeping ready." They had passed the first step in becoming military pilots—learning how to fly airplanes. Davis reported that the men "were now eager for the second step—learning to fly in combat as legitimate members of Uncle Sam's Army Air Corps."

The squadron's orders finally arrived in March 1943. As the pilots boarded a train in Chehaw, Alabama, they began the long journey that would take them to North Africa. Benjamin said good-bye to Agatha, wondering if he would see her again. But his attention soon turned to the future. "I was embarking on a highly important mission," Davis

The airmen of the 99th Pursuit Squadron proudly wore this insignia of their unit.

said, "the outcome of which would affect the lives of all the men in my unit and possibly the future of millions of other black people in the United States." As squadron commander, Davis knew that people would be watching his performance to see if a black man could lead combat troops.

Weeks later, the pilots of the 99th arrived in the North African desert. For months, the Allies—American, Canadian, and British forces—had been battling German forces in Algeria, Morocco, and Tunisia. A few days after the 99th arrived, the last German soldiers in North Africa surrendered.

The Americans and their allies were preparing to invade Italy, across the Mediterranean Sea from Africa. The attack plans called for the 99th to play an important role.

On June 22, America's first black pilots flew their first combat mission. The small island of Pantelleria, off the Tunisian coast, was still controlled by the enemy. Gaining control of the island meant cutting off the shipping lanes to Italy, a strategy that would prevent the enemy from getting vital war supplies.

The pilots flew strafing missions, in which they came in low and showered the island's defenders with machine-gun bullets. They also flew bomber escort, grouping their attack planes around a heavy bomber to defend it from enemy planes. The pilots worked as a team, anxiously scanning the skies for German Me-109s and FW-190s, which could fly higher and faster than the American P-40s.

On June 11, 1943, the Allies captured Pantelleria. The 99th Pursuit Squadron received special praise from the area commander, Colonel J.R. Hawkins. "You have met the challenge of the enemy," Hawkins wrote to Davis. "There is every reason to believe that with more experience you will take your place in the battle line along with the best of them."

The Allied invasion of Sicily, a large island that is part of Italy, began on July 10. From the

Davis flew his first combat missions in P-39 (left) and P-40 aircraft.

sky, the 99th offered protection to troops landing on Sicily's coast and chased enemy fighter planes that tried to attack Navy ships.

During one bomber-escort mission, a group of enemy fighters dove into the 99th's cover formation. In the fierce battle that followed, Lieutenant Charles Hall became the first black flier to shoot down an enemy plane.

Nine days later, the men of the 99th moved their air base to Sicily. There, they enjoyed better living conditions as well as fruit and vegetables fresh from Sicily's farms. But the squadron's work remained difficult and dangerous.

The pilots flew a dozen missions a day, bombing railroad yards, factories, bridges, and airfields. On some busy days, the airmen of the 99th flew one mission, returned to the base for fresh ammunition, then took off again.

On September 3, 1943, Davis received surprising news. The Army called him back to the United States to command the 332nd Fighter Group, a unit which consisted of three squadrons of black pilots preparing for duty.

Benjamin Davis, Jr., arrived home to receive a second surprise—criticism of the performance and ability of the 99th.

Benjamin Davis, Jr. wore this insignia as commander of the 332nd Fighter Group.

SPIT FIRE

Colonel William Momyer, a commander in the Mediterranean, had submitted a negative report on the 99th's operations and the skill, courage, and dedication of its pilots. Momyer reported that the 99th showed poor discipline, failed to operate as a team, and panicked under fire.

Another Army officer had added a comment of his own to Momyer's report. "The Negro type has not the proper reflexes to make a first-class fighter pilot," the officer wrote.

Momyer suggested that the 99th Squadron be removed from combat. The recommendation was approved by the commanding general of the Army Air Corps, who also proposed that the 332nd be given non-combat assignments and that plans for other black units be abandoned.

Benjamin Davis knew what such a recommendation meant. The Tuskegee experiment might be over. Davis also knew that the criticism was not based on the facts. "I was furious," he recalled. He met with a committee from the War Department to tell them his side of the story.

"The 99th had performed as well as any new fighter squadron, black or white," Davis told the committee. He did not tell the committee that the report was the product of racist attitudes toward black soldiers. "I had to adopt a quiet, reasoned approach," Davis said, "presenting the facts in a way that would appeal to fairness and win out over ignorance and racism."

The government decided to conduct its own study of the 99th. Davis was pleased when that report revealed "no significant general difference between this squadron and the balance of the P-40 squadrons in the Mediterranean." The men of the 99th continued to fly combat missions, and new black squadrons were trained for future operations.

Davis's new fighter group, the 332nd, flew a different plane, the P-39. Sleeker than the P-40, the P-39 had a smaller cockpit. Six-foot Benjamin Davis felt cramped when he climbed inside. "My head rubbed against the canopy," he said, "and I had to keep my back bowed."

On January 3, 1944, the 332nd Fighter Group sailed for Italy. Soon after they came ashore, they learned that the 99th Fighter Squadron had won a major victory at Anzio, an Italian seaside town, on January 27 and 28. Pilots of the 99th Squadron had shot down 12 enemy fighters in two furious days of aerial combat.

The victory at Anzio made headlines across the United States. Many Americans read in *Time*

magazine that "any outfit would have been proud of the 99th's record." The men of the 99th "had finally gotten their big chance," the article continued, "and they knew what to do with it."

The 99th's critics, Benjamin Davis said, had been "silenced once and for all."

Along with this good news, however, Davis received a report that the 332nd had been assigned not to combat, but to coastal patrol. Its pilots were to guard harbors and escort supply ships.

Davis saw this as "a betrayal of everything we had been working for, and an intentional insult to me and my men." He kept his feelings to himself, though, and acted as if the group had been given an important job—"whether I believed it or not," he said.

The situation improved for the 332nd in March 1944, when they were transferred to bomber-escort duty. Davis himself was promoted to the rank of colonel. Then, in June, the 332nd moved to a new base at Ramitelli, a farming community on Italy's east coast. From Ramitelli, Davis led his pilots on a series of successful combat missions.

On one mission, the 332nd had to escort bombers as they attacked the German city of Munich. Munich was heavily protected by fighter planes and anti-aircraft guns. But the airmen completed their mission and shot down five enemy planes.

"Your formation flying and escort work is the best we have ever seen," a wing commander wrote the men of the 332nd upon their return.

The men of the 332nd earned a reputation for sticking with the bombers over a target—the most dangerous part of any bombing mission—and for safely escorting the bombers back to base. They became known as the "Red Tails" because the tails of their planes were painted red.

Davis received the Distinguished Flying Cross for leading the air mission over Munich. He stood

Davis received the Distinguished Flying Cross for leading air combat missions over Germany during World War II.

especially tall on that occasion as his father pinned the medal to his uniform.

Davis's men won victories, but they also took losses. Planes were shot down; men were killed. Within the close-knit group, Davis said, "the loss of fighter pilots was like the loss of family."

Some pilots, having bailed out of their planes, were captured by the Germans. The Germans could not understand the patriotism of the black airmen who fought for a country that denied them fair treatment. One captured black pilot, Lieutenant Harold Brown, recalled that the Germans asked him, "Why are you fellows so willing to fight for the United States?" The Germans told Brown, "We are considered enemies of the United States, yet our boys receive better treatment in the United States than you."

The war in Europe ended on June 8, 1945, and Davis said farewell to the men of the 332nd. "May all of us carry on in the future as nobly as we have in the past," he told the gathered pilots. Less than two weeks later, Davis was assigned to a new command—the 477th Bombardment Group, a unit of black pilots who were training for combat against the Japanese. Japan's surrender, however, brought World War II to an end.

Davis stands with his wife and father in a portrait taken during World War II.

The following March, the pilots of the 477th moved to Lockbourne Air Base near Columbus, Ohio. With Benjamin Davis in command, Lockbourne became the first black air base that was not controlled by white officers. Davis called the command "a milestone in the struggle for blacks to gain an equal footing in the armed services."

Davis demanded excellence from the people under his command in peace as well as in war. Lockbourne was soon known as one of the Army's top air bases. It was, said one inspection report, "the best-managed base in the Air Corps and could well be a model for other bases."

But life at Lockbourne had a more easy-going side, too. The staff formed an entertainment troupe, Operation Happiness, which gave shows at air bases throughout the world. (One of the entertainers, Daniel "Chappie" James, Jr., became the nation's first black four-star general.)

In September 1947, the Air Force became a distinct branch of the armed forces, separate from the Army. Less than a year later, President Harry S Truman signed Executive Order 9981, requiring the armed services to end segregation.

The integration of the Air Force was especially rewarding to Benjamin Davis. "Without a doubt," Davis reflected, "the wartime performance of the black fighter units I had commanded and the success of Lockbourne Air Force Base influenced the Air Force's decision to integrate."

In May 1949, the Air Force announced "that there shall be equality of treatment and opportunity for all persons in the Air Force without regard to race, color, religion, or national origin." Moving quickly to integrate black servicemen, the Air Force abolished its black units.

Black airmen took their places beside white servicemen and women. The era of the black fighter squadrons had come to an end.

Chapter 6

Reaching Out

The rapid integration of the U.S. armed services opened up new opportunities for Benjamin Davis. He was no longer held back by the unwritten rule that African-American officers could not command white troops. Through the 1950s and 1960s, Davis commanded pilots in the United States and overseas. He supervised Air Force operations in times of war and peace.

In 1950, Davis reported for duty at the Pentagon, the headquarters of the U.S. Defense Department. His new job, chief of the Fighter Branch, was to supervise the activities of the Air Force's fighter units.

Davis came to this position at a critical time. American forces had been sent to the Republic of Korea (South Korea) to fight off an invasion from

North Korea. U.S. Air Force pilots protected soldiers on the ground and bombed enemy positions. "Air power was the decisive factor in the Korean War," according to Davis.

The Korean War was America's first integrated military effort, the first war in which soldiers from different races fought side by side. Benjamin Davis could not help but be proud of the wartime role played by African Americans, including the many combat missions flown by black pilots from the old 99th and 332nd units.

"The record of the integrated services in Korea spoke for itself," according to a U.S. government report, "and it assured the nation and the world that the racially segregated American military was a thing of the past."

After Korea, Davis took on a series of overseas assignments. He commanded units in South Korea and Japan, and on the island nation of Taiwan. In Germany, as chief of staff of the 12th Air Force, Davis directed a peacetime force stationed in both Europe and North Africa.

Like his father, Davis discovered that he was able to escape racist attitudes when living overseas. "I found the respect I had been denied at home in other countries," he observed.

Davis climbs aboard an F-86 for a training mission in Korea in 1954.

Agatha enjoyed living in foreign countries as much as her husband did. She had a deep interest in the people and customs of other lands. As they reached out to meet new people, the Davises made true friends regardless of race or culture.

One of these new friends was a woman who taught Benjamin and Agatha some of the traditions of the Japanese people. The Davises learned, for instance, how the Japanese view cherry blossoms. As they watch the progress of the blossoms from bud to full flower and then to withering petals, the Japanese people think of the human life cycle— birth, maturity, and death.

The couple particularly enjoyed watching the "expressions of serenity, happiness, worship, and sheer joy on Japanese faces during *sakura*, cherry blossom viewing," Davis recalled.

Promoted to brigadier general, Davis inspects the Far East Air Force headquarters in Tokyo.

It was in Japan that Davis learned that he had been promoted to the rank of brigadier general. When he hurried home to tell Agatha the news, he saw to his surprise that his Japanese neighbors had already heard about the promotion. They had posted signs around the Davises' house welcoming the neighborhood's first general.

Benjamin and Agatha enjoyed taking part in the traditions of other cultures and sharing their own customs with their foreign hosts. In Taiwan, Agatha wore the high-collared dresses favored by Taiwanese women. On Christmas Eve, the Davises introduced their Taiwanese friends to the custom of caroling.

In Germany, the American couple "ate, drank, and made merry" with German families over the holidays, Davis reported, "getting to know, understand, and like them better in the process."

While stationed in Germany, Davis traveled to Italy, hoping to see the old airfields from which he had flown in World War II. After more than 20 years, however, most of the old bases were overgrown. "All I could see were fields of waving grain," Davis said.

While the Davises managed to escape racism overseas, black Americans fought for equality at

In the 1960s, Martin Luther King, Jr., led the country in a struggle against racism.

home. In the 1950s and 1960s, their protests led to historic Supreme Court rulings that outlawed racial discrimination.

The Davises followed the news from America closely. They were distressed as peaceful protests met with violence. They were "deeply moved" as the Reverend Martin Luther King, Jr., spoke of his dream of a country where blacks and whites would "sit down together at the table of brotherhood."

In April 1968, Benjamin Davis was at Clark Air Force Base in the Philippines. There, he heard the news that Martin Luther King, Jr., had been shot to death in Memphis, Tennessee.

In the days that followed, Davis followed the reports of widespread racial violence in cities across the United States. "It was difficult for Agatha and me," he said, "to understand this tragic violence that seemed to dominate both blacks and whites in the United States."

Davis was in the Philippines to command the 13th Air Force. America was at war again, this time in Vietnam. Davis's job was to keep the airfields of Vietnam supplied with jets and bombers.

In Vietnam, African-American soldiers fought in every branch of the U.S. military and in every capacity. No longer restricted to menial jobs, blacks were pilots, engineers, and medics. By the end of the war, there were 12 black generals in the Army, three in the Air Force, and one black admiral in the Navy. Of the 277 Medals of Honor awarded in the war, 20 went to black soldiers.

A black American faces heavy shelling to rescue a wounded soldier. More than 50,000 blacks fought in the Vietnam War.

But progress was not the same thing as equality. Though blacks made up 9 percent of the armed forces during the Vietnam era, they accounted for only 2 percent of the officers. They were more likely to take part in combat than whites; they were more at risk of injury and death. At one point in the war, blacks accounted for 23 percent of combat deaths although they made up only 11 percent of the population of the United States.

In 1968, Davis was reassigned to MacDill Air Force Base, near Tampa, Florida. He had reached the rank of major general. After serving for 33 years in the armed forces, General Davis decided that the time had come to retire.

Finally, in February 1970, Benjamin Davis, Jr., put away his Air Force uniform. Looking back on his military career, Davis had no regrets. "I could never have had another career to compare with what I had experienced in the Air Force," he said.

Chapter 7

New
Directions

"It was like stepping into the uncharted sea of the civilian world," General Benjamin Davis said upon his retirement.

It was a time to branch out in new directions, a time to meet new challenges. "I had welcomed challenges all my life," Davis remarked. He was not about to stop welcoming them.

At first, he took a job as director of public safety for the city of Cleveland, Ohio. Benjamin Davis had happy memories of his high-school years in Cleveland and looked forward to working for Carl Stokes, the city's first black mayor. He was eager to help the people of Cleveland, a city that was troubled by racial tension and violence.

A new job brought him back to Washington, D.C. In September 1970, John Volpe, the Secretary of Transportation, asked for Davis's assistance. He needed someone to help combat the problem of "skyjacking," the hijacking of commercial airliners. During the 1960s, there had been more than 100 skyjackings in the United States.

Benjamin and Agatha settled in an apartment in Arlington, Virginia, across the Potomac River from Washington, D.C. From the ninth-floor windows, they looked out upon the Lincoln Memorial, the Washington Monument, and the white dome of the U.S. Capitol.

Soon after the Davises arrived in Washington, D.C., Benjamin Davis's father died at age 93. The Davis family gathered for the funeral at Arlington National Cemetery, the country's largest military cemetery. "During the funeral I thought about my long and happy relationship with this remarkable man," Benjamin Davis, Jr., wrote. "I found myself overcome with grief."

But Davis had an assignment to complete, and he soon turned his attention to the problem of skyjacking. He started a training program for sky marshals (police officers who ride on airplanes) and increased security at airports.

As in the Air Force, he demanded good performance from the people who worked for him—

and he got results. Davis's special assistant at the Department of Transportation, John Daniels, put it this way: "Air piracy had the nation scared. The aviation and law enforcement people were fighting over solutions and accomplishing nothing. Enter General Davis; nine months later, exit problem."

The number of skyjackings declined drastically once Davis's measures were in place. Not long after he took on the challenge of keeping America's skies safe, Davis was able to report that "skyjacking in the United States had become a thing of the past."

Davis next turned his attention to traffic safety. Studies had shown that by lowering the speed limit on American highways, thousands of lives could be saved each year. Davis earned the nickname

In 1970, Davis chats with President Richard Nixon and Secretary of Transportation John Volpe about his new job as head of a program to stop skyjackers.

"Mr. 55" as he traveled throughout the country calling for a 55-mile-per-hour speed limit. In 1973, the speed limit was lowered to 55. One year later, the traffic death toll dropped by 9,100.

When Davis had time off, he and Agatha liked to be with their families. In 1976, they invited their relatives to Arlington for Christmas. Agatha spoke to the gathering of loved ones.

"To our family each one brought the one he and she loved," she said. "And so we grew and grew and grew. Now we are many, each leading a different kind of life but held together by the love we have for each other."

Benjamin Davis had lived a life very different from that of most Americans. His friends urged him to write a book about his life. At first, Davis resisted the idea. Writing the book would mean reliving painful memories, such as his treatment at West Point and Fort Benning.

But Agatha encouraged him to do it, and she offered to help. In a bedroom of their apartment, she organized the many letters, newspaper articles, and official papers that her husband had saved over the years.

While doing research for the book, the couple traveled to West Point. The military academy had

Davis, pictured here in 1971, stayed in public service after he retired from the military.

72

Colin Powell was appointed chairman of the Joint Chiefs of Staff in 1989.

changed in the years since Davis was a cadet. Black cadets were common, and women were now admitted. In 1973, the Honor Committee had ended the practice of silencing.

The Davises visited Benjamin's old room, his classrooms, and the mess hall. They saw the basement where a young Benjamin Davis had overheard the other cadets talking about him years ago. They went to the library where they had spent many cold and rainy Saturday afternoons.

Everyone at West Point was friendly and helpful to the Davises, cadets and teachers alike. "It was the best week I ever spent at West Point," Benjamin told Agatha.

In the years since Benjamin Davis retired from the Air Force, African Americans have gained new opportunities in the military. In 1989, Davis witnessed the appointment of an African American, General Colin L. Powell, to the most important military post in the nation—chairman of the Joint Chiefs of Staff.

"I was extremely proud that Colin Powell had been able to impress the people for whom he worked so favorably," Davis said. He looked upon Powell's appointment as a "beacon of opportunity for other people."

Throughout his long career, Benjamin Davis has accepted tough challenges and turned them into opportunities. As a cadet at West Point, he stood up to cruel treatment and graduated with high grades. In an Army that did not train black pilots, he held onto his dream of flying—and he flew to victory in World War II. Davis's efforts helped to win battles in Korea and Vietnam. And in his years with the Department of Transportation, he made the skies and roads safer for all Americans.

As he enters his ninth decade, Benjamin O. Davis, Jr., can look back with pride on a life lived according to the West Point motto that inspired him so many years ago. He has truly devoted himself to duty, honor, and country.

Chronology:

African Americans in the U.S. Armed Forces

1770	On March 5, Crispus Attucks, a former slave, is among the first to die in the "Boston Massacre."
1776-1781	7,000 African-American soldiers and sailors take part in the Revolutionary War.
1776	On January 16, the Continental Congress agrees to enlist free blacks.
1812-1815	Black soldiers and sailors fight against British troops at such critical battles as Lake Erie and New Orleans.
1862-1865	186,000 African-American soldiers serve in black regiments during the Civil War; 38,000 black soldiers lose their lives in more than 400 battles.
1862	On July 17, the U.S. Congress approves the enlistment of black soldiers.
1865	On March 13, the Confederate States of America begins to accept black recruits.
1866-1890	Units of black soldiers, referred to as Buffalo Soldiers, are formed as part of the U.S. Army.
1872	On September 21, John H. Conyers becomes the first African American admitted to the U.S. Naval Academy.
1877	On June 15, Henry O. Flipper becomes the first African American to graduate from West Point.
1914-1918	More than 400,000 African Americans serve in the U.S. armed forces during the First World War.

On May 15, two black soldiers, Henry Johnson and Needham Roberts become the first Americans to receive the French Medal of Honor (*Croix de Guerre*).	1918
In June, Benjamin O. Davis, Jr., graduates from West Point, the first black American to do so in the twentieth century.	1936
Benjamin O. Davis, Sr., becomes the first African-American general in the active Regular Army.	1940
American forces in World War II include more than a million African-American men and women.	1941-1945
On March 25, the Army Air Corps forms its first black unit, the 99th Pursuit Squadron.	1941
On August 24, Colonel Benjamin O. Davis, Jr., is made commander of the 99th Pursuit Squadron.	1942
On January 27 and 28, the airmen of the 99th Pursuit Squadron score a major victory against enemy fighters at the Italian seaside town of Anzio.	1944
On February 2, President Harry S Truman signs Executive Order 9981, ordering an end to segregation in the U.S. armed forces.	1948
Black and white forces fight side by side in Korea as separate black fighting units are disbanded.	1950-1953
Twenty African-American soldiers are awarded the Congressional Medal of Honor during the Vietnam War.	1965-1973
On April 28, Samuel L. Gravely becomes the first black admiral in the history of the U.S. Navy.	1971
In August, Daniel "Chappie" James becomes the first African American to achieve the rank of four-star general.	1975
On October 3, Colin Powell becomes the first African-American chairman of the Joint Chiefs of Staff.	1989
100,000 African-American men and women are sent to the Middle East during the Persian Gulf conflict.	1990-1991

Index

Bibliography

Daniels, John E. Letter to the editor. *The Washington Post*, February 21, 1991.

Davis, Benjamin O., Jr. *Benjamin O. Davis, Jr.: American*. Washington, D.C.: Smithsonian Institution Press, 1991.

Davis, Benjamin O., Jr. Memorial Day Lecture at the National Archives, Washington, D.C., May 29, 1991.

Glatthaar, Joseph. Review of *Benjamin O. Davis Jr.: American*, by Benjamin O. Davis, Jr. *The Washington Post Book Review*, March 17, 1991.

Greene, Robert Ewell. *Black Defenders of America: 1775-1973*. Chicago: Johnson Publishing, 1974.

Scott, EdRoyal. *Profiles of Black Achievers: 1930-1950*. Los Angeles: Authors Unlimited, 1988.

Wakin, Edward. *Black Fighting Men in U.S. History*. New York: Lothrop, Lee & Shepherd, 1971.

Washington Past and Present. Washington, D.C.: The United States Capitol Historical Society, 1987.

Weinraub, Judith. "The Long, Lonely Flight of General Benjamin Davis." *The Washington Post*, February 4, 1991.

Williams, Juan. *Eyes on the Prize: America's Civil Rights Years 1954-1965*. New York: Viking Penguin, 1987.